CW00530165

JOHANNA SPYRI

Heidi

Retold by Anne Collins

**EAL DEPARTMENT
YARDLEYS SCHOOL**

MACMILLAN

PRE-INTERMEDIATE LEVEL

Founding Editor: John Milne

The Macmillan Readers provide a choice of enjoyable reading materials for learners of English. The series is published at six levels – Starter, Beginner, Elementary, Pre-intermediate, Intermediate and Upper.

Level Control
Information, structure and vocabulary are controlled to suit the students' ability at each level.

The number of words at each level:

Starter	about 300 basic words
Beginner	about 600 basic words
Elementary	about 1100 basic words
Pre-intermediate	about 1400 basic words
Intermediate	about 1600 basic words
Upper	about 2200 basic words

Vocabulary
Some difficult words and phrases in this book are important for understanding the story. Some of these words are explained in the story, some are shown in the pictures, and others are marked with a number like this: ...3. Words with a number are explained in the Glossary at the end of the book.

Answer Keys
Answer Keys for the *Points for Understanding* and *Exercises* sections can be found at www.macmillanenglish.com

Contents

A Note About The Author

Johanna Spyri was born in Switzerland, on 12th July, 1827. She grew up in Hirzel – a village near Zurich. When she was a child, Johanna was called Hanni. Her family name was Heusser. Hanni had three sisters and two brothers. Her father was a doctor, and her mother wrote songs and poems. The Heussers lived in a little white house which stood on a hill. The hill was covered with trees and all around it, there were high mountains.

Hanni loved her home and she was a happy, healthy child. In summer, she spent most of her time outdoors with her brothers and sisters. She was very interested in plants, animals and birds. Sometimes she took care of the family's goats while they ate the grass on the mountains.

In 1852, Hanni married Bernhard Spyri, a young law student. Hanni and Bernhard went to live in Zurich. They had many friends who were writers and artists. Hanni enjoyed writing stories too. She had a son, and wrote stories for him. Unfortunately, Hanni's son did not have good health. He was weak and had many illnesses. He died in 1884, aged twenty-nine. Soon after his death, Bernhard died too. This was a very unhappy time for Hanni.

After the Franco-Prussian War (1870–71), there were many injured[1] soldiers in Switzerland. Hanni used money from her stories to help these men. She wrote about fifty novels, but *Heidi* was her most famous and successful book. It was published in 1880. In 1884, *Heidi* was translated into English, and it became very popular in Britain and America.

Johanna Spyri spent a lot of her time helping poor people and visiting schools. She died on 7th July, 1901.

A Note About This Story

The heroine[2] of this story – a little Swiss girl named Heidi – goes to live with her grandfather. His home is a little house high on a mountain. Heidi's grandfather is a sad and angry man, but he soon begins to love Heidi.

In this book, Johanna Spyri describes the beautiful Swiss Alps and writes about the people, animals, plants and birds who live there. But *Heidi* is about other things as well. It is about loneliness, sadness, friendship and happiness. Little Heidi has a loving heart and she is very kind. She brings joy to many people.

A Picture Dictionary

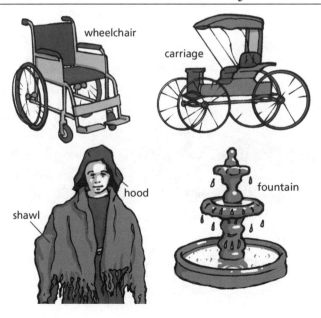

wheelchair

carriage

hood

shawl

fountain

fir trees

hawk

peak

mountain (alp)

mountainside

pasture

hut

ledge

valley — churchtower

loft

slope

hay

ravine

bushes

rock

stall

sledge

shovel

ladder

shutter

path

goat

stove

cooking pot

candle

tools
(hammer, nails)

pipe

stick

mug

bench

basket

bundle

tablecloth

hurdy-gurdy

inkwell

rug

ink

tobacco

stool

sack

gun

kittens

6

The People in This Story

Dörfli

Heidi ('Adelheid')

Detie

Uncle Alp (Grandfather)

Peter

Bridget

Grannie

7

Frankfurt

Mr Sesemann

Clara Sesemann

Mrs Sesemann
(Grandmamma)

Miss Rottenmeier

Sebastian

Mr Usher

Doctor Classen

1

Heidi and her Grandfather

In winter, the high peaks of the Swiss Alps are completely covered with snow. But in spring and summer, the snow disappears from the slopes and valleys. And you can see grass and pretty flowers everywhere.

The small town of Mayenfeld lies in a valley in the east of Switzerland. A tall mountain rises up behind the town.

One morning in June, a tall young woman was walking slowly up the mountain path. The young woman's name was Detie. In her left hand, Detie carried a bundle of clothes. Her right hand was holding the hand of a little girl. It was a warm, sunny day but the little girl was wearing two woollen dresses, one on top of the other. She also had woollen stockings[3] on her legs and boots on her feet. A long red scarf[4] was tied tightly around her body.

Halfway up the side of the mountain, Detie and the little girl came to a small village. This was Dörfli, the place where Detie had been born. As they went through the village, a woman called out to her.

'Detie!' she shouted. 'Let me walk with you!'

A large woman with a pleasant face came out of a house. This was Barbie, an old friend of Detie's.

'Is this your sister's child?' asked Barbie.

'Yes,' replied Detie. 'This is my niece, Heidi. She's five years old. When my sister died a few years ago, I had to take care of Heidi.'

'But where are you taking her?' asked Barbie.

'I'm taking her to Uncle Alp's house,' replied Detie. 'Uncle Alp is Heidi's grandfather. She'll have to stay with him now.'

'Detie!' said Barbie. 'You can't leave the child with *Uncle Alp*! He doesn't know how to care for children!'

'He must take care of Heidi now,' said Detie. 'I'm going to live in Germany because I have a new job in Frankfurt. *I* can't take care of Heidi any more.'

Barbie looked up towards the top of the mountain.

'Uncle Alp lives all alone up there,' she said. 'He doesn't like people and people don't like him. He always looks so unhappy and angry.'

Detie turned round. 'Where's Heidi?' she asked.

Barbie saw the child on the path below them and pointed.

'Look, she's down there, with Peter,' she said.

The little girl was with a young boy. There were several goats beside them.

'Peter will look after Heidi,' said Barbie. 'Now tell me more about Uncle Alp.'

'When Uncle Alp was young, he was very rich,' said Detie. 'He had one of the best farms in the country but he lost a lot of money. Uncle Alp had to sell the farm and leave Dörfli. Twelve years later, he came back with Tobias, his young son. When Tobias grew up, he married my sister, Adelheid. Tobias and Adelheid had a daughter – Heidi. But then Tobias was killed in an accident. Soon after this, Adelheid became ill and she died, too.

'Heidi came to live with me,' Detie went on. 'But I can't look after her now. So I'm taking her to Uncle Alp.'

The women, the children and the goats had reached a small wooden hut on the mountainside. This house was where Peter lived. He lived there with his mother and grandmother. Peter's father and grandfather were both dead.

Peter was eleven years old and he worked as a goatherd. He looked after goats. Every morning in summer, he went down to Dörfli and fetched the villagers' goats. Then he took the animals high up the mountain. He led them to a pasture where there was fresh new grass. Every evening, Peter took the goats back to the villagers' homes.

Barbie said goodbye to Detie and went into the hut. She wanted to visit Bridget, Peter's mother.

Detie climbed further up the mountain. After about fifteen minutes, she stopped to rest. Peter and the goats were on the path above her. Detie looked around. Where was Heidi?

Heidi was far below them. The little girl was very hot and tired in her heavy clothes. She sat down and pulled off her stockings and boots. Then she took off the thick scarf and her two woollen dresses. She put all the clothes carefully in a pile on the ground. Now she was wearing only a thin cotton dress. She felt very happy and free. She ran after Peter and the goats.

Detie waited on the steep[5] path for her niece.

'What have you done, Heidi?' she said angrily. 'Where are your woollen dresses? Where is your scarf, and where are your new boots?'

Heidi pointed down to the pile of clothes that was many metres below them.

'There they are,' she said. 'I don't need them.'

'Peter, run and fetch Heidi's clothes!' said Detie. She held out a coin towards him. 'Look,' she said. 'I'll give you this penny.'

Peter ran down the path quickly. He picked up the clothes and ran back to Heidi and Detie. Then he took the money from Detie and put it in his pocket.

'Now, Peter. Please carry the clothes to Uncle Alp's hut,' said Detie, and she began to climb up the path again. Heidi and Peter followed her.

After about an hour, they came to Uncle Alp's hut. The little house stood on a ledge which was high on the side of the mountain. The old man had a wonderful view from his

11

home. He could see right down the valley to Dörfli. Three
old fir trees, with big branches[6], grew next to the hut. The
ground rose up steeply behind the trees, to the top of the
mountain.

Uncle Alp was sitting on a wooden bench outside the
hut. He was smoking his pipe and looking at the view.

Heidi ran up to the old man and held out her hand.

'Hello, Grandfather,' she said.

'What did you say?' asked the old man. He stared at the little girl, and Heidi stared back at him.

'Good morning, Uncle Alp,' said Detie. 'This is Heidi, Tobias's daughter.'

'Why is she here?' the old man asked.

'I've taken care of Heidi for four years,' said Detie. 'But I can't look after her any more. I've got to go away. I have got a job in Germany. Heidi is your granddaughter and she has no other relatives. If anything bad happens to Heidi, you'll be in a lot of trouble.'

The old man stood up. 'Go away and don't ever come back here!' he said angrily.

'Very well,' said Detie quickly. She turned to her niece.

'Goodbye, Heidi,' she said. Then she ran down the mountain. She did not stop until she came to Dörfli.

When Detie had gone, Uncle Alp sat down on the bench again. Heidi walked around the hut. She listened to the sound of the wind in the trees and liked it very much. Then she came back and stood in front of her grandfather.

'I want to see inside the hut,' she said.

'Very well,' he said. 'Bring your things with you.'

Heidi picked up the bundle and the clothes and followed the old man.

Inside the hut, there was only one big room. Heidi saw a table and a chair in the middle of the room, and a bed in one corner. Opposite the bed, there was an iron stove. A big cooking pot was hanging above the stove.

Uncle Alp opened a door which was in one wall. Behind the door, there was a large cupboard. Some of Uncle Alp's clothes were hanging inside the cupboard. There were also shelves with plates, cups and glasses on them. On the highest shelf, there was bread, meat and cheese.

'Where shall I sleep?' asked Heidi.

'Sleep wherever you like,' replied Uncle Alp.

13

Heidi turned and looked at her grandfather's bed again. On the wall near the bed, she saw a ladder, and she climbed up it. At the top of the ladder, Heidi could see into a loft. This long, narrow room had a high ceiling and it was full of soft, dry hay. Last summer, Peter and Uncle Alp had cut some long, sweet grass from the pastures. After the grass had dried in the sun, they had put it in the loft.

In the wall at the end of the loft, there was a round hole. Heidi looked through this window and saw Dörfli, far away, at the bottom of the valley.

'Grandfather, I'll sleep here,' she said happily. 'It's a wonderful place. I'll make my bed in the hay.'

Uncle Alp climbed down the ladder and went to the cupboard. He found a large piece of material and a heavy sack[7]. He took them up to the loft and put them on top of the hay.

'Thank you,' said Heidi. 'Now I have a sheet and a warm cover for my bed.'

They went down the ladder and Uncle Alp went to the stove. He picked up a fork with a long handle. On the end of the fork, he put a large piece of cheese. Then he held the fork near the fire in the stove. Soon, the golden yellow cheese became soft. It smelt delicious.

Heidi ran to the cupboard. She took out two plates, two knives and the loaf of bread. She put them on the table.

'Good,' said her grandfather. 'But there's something missing.'

Heidi thought for a moment, then she ran to the cupboard again. She brought a mug and a glass, and put them on the table too.

'Where are you going to sit?' asked Uncle Alp.

Heidi picked up a wooden stool but it was too low. When Heidi sat on the seat, she could not reach the table. Uncle Alp got up and pushed his own chair in front of Heidi's stool. Then he filled the mug with milk and put it on the chair. Finally, he put a piece of bread and the hot, toasted cheese on a plate for her.

'Now you have a table,' he said. 'Drink. Eat.'

Heidi drank her milk and ate her bread and cheese. The meal was delicious.

After they had finished eating, Uncle Alp fetched his tools and some wood. He made a chair for Heidi.

In the afternoon, a strong wind started to blow through the trees. Heidi ran and jumped with happiness. She loved the sound of the wind. Suddenly they heard a loud, sharp whistle[8].

'Ah! Here comes Peter and the goats!' said Heidi's grandfather. 'He always whistles when he arrives.'

Uncle Alp had two goats. They lived in a stall – a small room behind the hut. Every morning, Uncle Alp's goats went to the pasture with Peter and the villagers' goats. Every evening, Peter brought his goats back to the hut.

Now, two goats – one brown and one white – left the herd and ran towards the old man. Uncle Alp was holding a little salt, which the goats loved.

The old man filled a mug with milk from the white goat. He gave the mug to Heidi. He also gave her some bread.

'Eat this and drink the milk,' he said. 'Then go to bed and sleep well.'

'What are the goats' names?' asked Heidi.

'The white one is Daisy, and the brown one is Dusky,' he replied. Then he took the goats to their stall.

'Good night, Daisy! Good night, Dusky!' called Heidi.

That night, the wind blew very strongly. It shook the whole hut.

'Perhaps Heidi is afraid of the wind,' thought her grandfather. He climbed up the ladder and looked into the loft. Moonlight shone through the window onto Heidi's face. She was sleeping peacefully.

15

2

A Day with the Goats

When Heidi woke next morning, the sun was shining brightly. She jumped out of her bed and got dressed. Peter was waiting outside the hut with the herd of goats as Uncle Alp brought Daisy and Dusky from their stall.

'Do you want to go to the pasture with Peter today?' he asked Heidi.

'Yes, please, Grandfather,' she said.

'Peter, give me your bag,' said Uncle Alp.

The old man put a mug, a large piece of bread, and some cheese into the bag.

'This is Heidi's dinner,' he said to the boy. 'Fill her mug with milk from my goats. Take care of my granddaughter. The mountain slopes are steep and the paths are dangerous. Don't let her fall into the ravine.'

The sun shone in the blue sky and pretty mountain flowers covered the ground. Heidi ran about excitedly. She picked lots of flowers and carried them in her skirt.

'Come on!' called Peter. 'You've got enough flowers now. Don't pick any more.'

At last, they reached the pasture and the goats began to eat the sweet grass. Only a few bushes and some small trees grew on the highest slopes of the mountain. The top of the mountain was bare rock.

It was warm and peaceful on the pasture. Peter lay on the grass and very soon he was asleep. Heidi sat down beside Peter and looked around. Beside her, there was an extremely steep slope. This was the ravine where the ground dropped down many thousands of metres, to the valley, far below. On the other side of the valley, there was a high mountain. Its peak was covered in snow.

16

Suddenly, Heidi heard a loud cry. She looked up and saw a big bird flying high above her head.

'Peter! Peter!' she shouted.

Peter woke up and Heidi pointed at the bird.

'What is it?' she asked.

The bird flew in large circles and then disappeared near the top of the mountain.

'That's a hawk,' said Peter. 'It's gone home to its nest.'

'Let's climb up and see where the hawk lives,' said Heidi.

'Oh, no,' replied Peter. 'Its nest is much too high. Even the goats can't climb up there.'

After a few minutes, Peter started whistling and shouting. When the goats heard his voice they came to him. He began to lead them down the path. When they reached the lower pasture, Peter opened his bag and took out all the bread and cheese. Heidi's pieces of bread and cheese were much larger than his own dinner. Peter went to Daisy and filled Heidi's mug with the white goat's milk.

'It's dinner time,' he said. 'Sit down and eat.'

'Is the milk for me?' Heidi asked.

'Yes,' he replied. 'And this bread and cheese.'

Heidi drank the milk, but she only ate a little of the bread. Then she gave the cheese and the rest of her bread to Peter. He looked surprised and pleased.

'What are the names of the goats?' Heidi asked.

Peter pointed to each goat and told her its name. There was Big Turk and Finch, Dusky and Daisy, Spot and Snowflake. Snowflake, a beautiful little white goat, was making sad little noises. Heidi ran up to Snowflake and put her arms round the goat's neck.

'Why are you crying, Snowflake?' Heidi asked.

'She's missing her mother,' said Peter. 'Her owner sold Snowflake's mother to someone in Mayenfeld.'

'Don't cry, Snowflake,' said Heidi. 'I'll be up here every

day now. You can come to me if you feel lonely.'

When Peter had finished eating, he took Heidi and the goats to the high pasture again. Peter sat on the grass and watched the herd. Then suddenly, he jumped up and ran to the edge of the ravine. Finch, the smallest goat, was going to fall! Peter stretched out his hand and held one of Finch's legs. Then the boy slipped and almost fell into the ravine himself! Finch tried to get away from Peter. And the boy could not get up unless he let go of Finch's leg.

'Heidi!' shouted Peter. 'Come and help!'

Heidi held some grass near to Finch. The little goat turned its head towards Heidi and ate the grass from her hand.

At last Peter got up, and both children pulled Finch from the edge of the ravine. Peter was angry. He picked up his stick to hit the little goat.

'No! Don't beat Finch!' said Heidi. 'He's frightened, that's all. Please don't hurt him.'

Peter was so surprised that he dropped the stick.

'I won't beat him, if you promise to give me some of your food tomorrow,' he said.

'You can have my food every day,' said Heidi. 'But you must never beat Finch, or any of the goats, again.'

'All right,' said Peter.

It was getting late. Heidi sat quietly and watched the sun going down in the sky. As the sun set, its wonderful golden light shone on the grass and flowers.

Suddenly Heidi jumped up. The setting sun had coloured the mountain peaks. They were now bright red – the colour of flames.

'Peter! A fire!' shouted Heidi. 'The mountains are burning and the snow and sky are burning too!'

'There isn't a fire,' said Peter. 'The sky and the mountains always become red in the evenings.'

'What are the mountains' names?' asked Heidi.

'Mountains don't have names,' Peter replied.

At last, the sun went down behind the mountains. Heidi felt very sad as the beautiful colour disappeared.

'It's time to go home,' said Peter. He whistled and called the goats. And they all started to walk down the mountain.

Heidi sat on her new high chair and ate her supper.

'Grandfather, why haven't the mountains got names?' she asked.

'But they *do* have names,' replied the old man. 'Describe a mountain to me and I'll tell you its name.'

Heidi described the mountain with its peak covered in snow.

'That's Scesaplana,' said Grandfather.

Next, Heidi pointed to one of the mountains behind the hut. This mountain had two sharp peaks of rock.

'What is the name of *that* mountain?' she asked.

'That's Falkniss,' replied Grandfather.

When Heidi described other mountains, Uncle Alp told her their names too.

'Did you have a good time today?' he asked.

'Oh, yes,' said Heidi. 'The best thing was when the mountain began to burn. But Peter said that there wasn't a fire. What happened, Grandfather?'

'That's how the sun says goodnight to the mountains,' said Grandfather. 'It shines that beautiful red light over them. Then the mountains remember the sun until the next morning.'

3

A Visit to Grannie

All through that summer, Heidi went to the high pasture with Peter and the goats. She played happily in the warm sun and her skin became golden brown. But when autumn came, the wind began to blow strongly.

'You must stay at home from now on,' Grandfather told her. 'The wind could easily blow you off the mountain.'

Heidi was happy in the hut. She loved the sound of the wind in the fir trees and she loved to watch her grandfather making things from wood.

Soon it was winter and suddenly, the weather became very cold. Now Heidi was happy to wear her thick woollen dress, warm stockings and boots. Then one night, snow started to fall. It snowed for many hours.

The next morning, Peter could not take the goats up the mountain. Everything – the grass, trees, bushes, rocks

– was covered by thick snow. Heidi watched the big, white snowflakes falling faster and faster to the ground.

On the second day of the snowstorm, Heidi and Grandfather could not get out of the hut because the snow covered the doors and windows. Grandfather worked hard for several hours removing[9] the snow from the walls of the hut with a large shovel.

In the afternoon, Heidi and Grandfather sat down by the stove. Suddenly, someone knocked on the door very loudly. Grandfather opened it, and there was Peter. His boots and clothes were covered with snow.

'Hello,' he said, walking to the warm stove.

'Well, Peter,' said the old man, 'how are your lessons?'

'Lessons?' said Heidi.

'Yes,' said Grandfather. 'In the winter, Peter has to go to school. He must learn to read and write.'

So Peter told Heidi about the school while Uncle Alp prepared a meal. When Peter saw the bread and meat, he opened his eyes wide. He did not usually get so much food for his supper.

Slowly the sky began to get dark and Peter stood up.

'I must leave now,' he said. 'Thank you for supper. I'll come again next Sunday. Oh! And I have a message for Heidi from my grandmother – Grannie. Please will you visit her? Goodbye.'

———

Three days passed and the snow was very soft and deep. But on the fourth day, the weather became extremely cold. The snow froze until it was as hard as iron.

'The sun's shining today,' said Heidi. 'I must go and visit Peter's Grannie.'

Grandfather went up to the loft and took the sack from Heidi's bed. 'Come on, then,' he said.

Outside, everything was white and shining.

21

'Look at the trees!' cried Heidi. The tall fir trees were covered with bright snow.

Grandfather pulled a big wooden sledge out of the goats' stall. He wrapped the sack around Heidi's body to keep her warm. Then he sat on the sledge and put Heidi in front of him. When he pushed his feet on the ground, the sledge moved over the hard snow. Soon they were travelling down the mountain, faster and faster until they stopped outside Peter's hut.

'Go and visit Peter's grandmother,' said Grandfather. 'Come home when the sun starts to set.' Then he turned and began to walk back up the mountain pulling the sledge behind him.

Heidi opened the door of Peter's hut and went inside. She was in a room which had a low ceiling. A woman was sitting at a table and repairing[10] a jacket. This was Bridget, Peter's mother. She made and repaired clothes. An older woman was sitting in the corner of the room. Heidi went up to her.

'Hello, Grannie,' she said. 'Here I am.'

The old woman stretched her hand towards Heidi. She reached out to touch Heidi's own hand, then held it tightly.

'Are you the child who is living with Uncle Alp?' she asked. 'Are you Heidi?'

'Yes, I am.'

'Bridget, what does the girl look like?' asked Grannie, turning her head towards Peter's mother.

'Heidi is thin, like her mother was,' said Bridget. 'But her mother had blue eyes and Heidi's got black eyes. Heidi has curly hair, like her father Tobias, and Uncle Alp.'

Heidi looked round the room. 'Grannie, one of the wooden shutters[11] outside your window is loose,' she said. 'The shutter is hitting the window. It'll break the glass. Look!'

'I can't see it, but I can hear it,' said Grannie. 'When the wind blows, the shutter makes a terrible noise. At night, I can't sleep because I'm frightened. I worry that the hut will fall down because so many things are broken.'

'Why can't you see the shutter?' asked Heidi.

'I'm blind[12], child,' said Grannie. 'I can't see at all.'

When Heidi heard this she became very upset and started to cry.

'My dear,' said Grannie. 'I can't see, but I can hear. It's good to hear a friendly voice like yours. Tell me about your grandfather and your life up on the mountain. What do you do there?'

Heidi slowly dried her tears. 'I'll tell Grandfather about your problems,' she told Grannie. 'He can do anything. He'll repair your hut and he'll make you see again.'

Peter came into the room. He was surprised and pleased when he saw Heidi.

'Have you returned from school already?' asked Grannie. 'This afternoon has passed so quickly! How is your reading?'

'Just the same,' Peter replied.

'I wish that Peter could read,' said Grannie to Heidi. 'I want him to learn. There are books on the shelf above my chair. I want Peter to read them to me, but reading is too difficult for him.'

It was becoming dark so Bridget lit a candle.

'It will be night soon,' said Heidi. 'I must go.'

'Peter will go with you,' said Grannie.

Heidi began to run quickly up the mountain and Peter followed her. But Uncle Alp was already coming down the mountain towards them. He wrapped Heidi in the sack and carried her home in his arms.

'Grandfather,' said Heidi. 'Tomorrow, you must take your tools to Peter's hut. You must repair Grannie's shutter. It makes a terrible noise when the wind blows and Grannie is frightened at night. And can you help Grannie to see?'

'I can't help her to see,' said Grandfather. 'But I can repair the shutter.'

The next afternoon, Heidi and Uncle Alp went down to Peter's hut again. While Heidi spoke to Grannie, Grandfather repaired the shutter.

'Uncle Alp,' said Bridget. 'Thank you for helping us. Mother and I are very grateful. Please, will you come inside? My mother wants to thank you herself.'

'I'll repair your hut, but I won't come inside,' said Uncle Alp. Then he climbed up onto the roof and repaired some holes there too.

When the sun began to set, Heidi went to her grandfather. He wrapped her in the sack then carried her home, pulling the sledge behind him.

———

Heidi often visited Grannie that winter. She loved Grannie very much. The old, blind woman had been sad for many years but now she was happy. She loved Heidi's visits and often asked Bridget if Heidi looked well.

'She looks as healthy as a fresh red apple,' replied Bridget.

When the weather was fine, Grandfather took his tools down to Peter's hut and repaired the whole house. Now Grannie was no longer frightened by noises in the night.

4

Two Visitors

Two years passed. Heidi was now seven years old. Twice, Peter brought messages to Uncle Alp from the schoolteacher in Dörfli.

Uncle Alp, You must send Heidi to school, wrote the teacher. *Your granddaughter must be educated.*

But the old man did not want to send Heidi to the school. He wanted her to stay at home with him.

———

It was March. The long winter had almost passed. The sun was warmer and the snow was disappearing. One morning, Heidi saw a man standing outside the hut.

'Don't be afraid,' said the man kindly. 'You must be Heidi. Where's your grandfather?'

'He's inside,' said Heidi. 'He's making wooden spoons.'

The visitor was the pastor[13] from Dörfli. He lived and worked in the church in the village. Many years ago, Uncle Alp had also lived in Dörfli. At that time, he and the pastor had been neighbours.

'Good morning, pastor,' said Uncle Alp in surprise.

'I've come to talk to you about the child,' said the pastor. 'You must send her to school.'

'No,' said the old man. 'She'll grow up here with the goats and the birds. She'll be very happy here.'

'But she's not a goat, or a bird,' said the pastor. 'She's a little girl and she must learn to read and write. Why don't you come back to Dörfli next winter? Everyone will be friendly to you.'

'No,' said Uncle Alp. 'I won't send the child to school. And I won't come back to live in Dörfli.'

The pastor went away. But two days later, Heidi and her grandfather had another visitor. This time it was Detie, Heidi's aunt. Detie was wearing a fine dress and a hat with a feather.

'Heidi looks very well!' said Detie. 'But I've come to talk about a wonderful chance for her. I know a rich family in Frankfurt called the Sesemanns. Mr Sesemann's daughter, Clara, is an invalid[14]. She can't walk and she has to sit in a wheelchair. Her life is very boring. The family are looking for a friend for Clara. So I told them about Heidi and they want to meet her.'

'I'm not interested in this family,' said Uncle Alp.

'Heidi will soon be eight and she hasn't learnt anything,' said Detie. 'You won't let her go to school so she never meets anybody. You don't care about her.'

'All right!' shouted Uncle Alp. 'But if you take Heidi away, don't ever bring her back!' And he walked out of the hut.

'Heidi, get your clothes,' said Detie. 'Put on your hat and come with me.'

'No,' said Heidi. 'I'm not coming.'

'Your grandfather is angry,' said Detie. 'He doesn't want to see us again. He wants you to go with me. But if you don't like Frankfurt, you can come back here.'

'Can I come back this evening?' asked Heidi.

'No,' said Detie. 'Frankfurt is too far away. Today, we'll travel to Mayenfeld. Tomorrow, we'll go on to Frankfurt.'

Detie held Heidi's hand tightly and carried her bundle of clothes for her. Then she began to walk very fast, pulling Heidi along behind her. Halfway down the mountain path, they met Peter.

'Where are you going, Heidi?' he asked.

'I'm going to Frankfurt with my aunt,' replied Heidi. 'But I'll go to your house and see Grannie first.'

'No Heidi, there's no time to see Grannie,' said Detie. She held Heidi's hand more tightly and walked on.

Peter ran into the hut. 'Detie is taking Heidi away!' he shouted.

When she heard this, Grannie opened the window. 'Detie, please don't take the child away from us!' she called out sadly.

'I want to go and see Grannie!' cried Heidi, pulling at Detie's hand.

'We haven't got time to stop,' said Detie. 'We must get to the railway station or we will miss the train. You'll have a wonderful time in Frankfurt. When you come back here again, you can bring Grannie a present.'

'What kind of present?' asked Heidi.

'Perhaps she would like some nice soft rolls[15].'

'That's a good idea,' said Heidi. 'Grannie doesn't like the bread here because it's too hard. Let's hurry, Detie. Can we get to Frankfurt today? Then I can bring the rolls back for Grannie.'

When Detie and Heidi reached Dörfli, they passed through the village quickly. People tried to ask Detie questions, but she did not stop to answer.

From that day, Uncle Alp became very quiet. Sometimes he left his home on the mountain with cheese to sell. He took the round, yellow cheeses to the market in Mayenfeld. He passed through Dörfli carrying the cheeses in a basket on his back. But he did not speak to anyone and the villagers were afraid of him. He always carried a heavy stick and his face was cold and angry.

After Heidi left, Uncle Alp did not visit Grannie's hut any more. Grannie missed Heidi very much and the sad, old woman's days became long and empty.

5

A New Life

Detie took Heidi to the Sesemanns' big house in Frankfurt. Heidi was going to become Clara Sesemann's friend and companion[16]. Clara was an invalid and she did not go to school. She was taught her lessons at home and did not often leave the house.

Clara's mother was dead. So Mr Sesemann had a housekeeper to look after the house. This lady's name was Miss Rottenmeier.

Detie knocked hard on the front door and a servant opened it. His name was Sebastian and he wore a smart coat with big silver buttons.

'Can I see Miss Rottenmeier, please?' asked Detie. 'Here is my niece. She's going to be Miss Clara's companion.'

'You must call Tinette, the maid,' said Sebastian. He pointed to a bell on a table. 'Ring the bell.'

Detie rang the bell and Tinette came quickly into the hall. Then she took Detie and Heidi into a comfortable room with shelves full of books. This was the study, where Clara was taught her lessons. Miss Rottenmeier and Clara were already in the room. The young girl, who was sitting in a wheelchair, had blonde hair, a pale face and blue eyes.

Miss Rottenmeier was tall and thin, and she wore an ugly hat on her head. She stared at Heidi.

'What's your name?' she asked in a cold voice.

'Heidi,' replied the child in a clear voice.

'That's a strange name,' said Miss Rottenmeier.

'Her real name is Adelheid,' said Detie.

'She looks very young,' said Miss Rottenmeier. 'We wanted a child of the same age as Clara. Miss Clara is twelve.

How old is this child?'

'About ten years old, I think,' said Detie.

'I'll soon be eight,' said Heidi. 'Grandfather told me.'

'Not yet eight!' said Miss Rottenmeier. 'That's too young for Clara. Which books have you used in your lessons?'

'None,' said Heidi. 'I haven't learnt to read.'

'You haven't learnt to read!' said Miss Rottenmeier. She turned to Detie. 'Why did you bring this child here?' she asked angrily. 'She's younger than Clara and she can't even read!'

'I'm sorry, but I have to go now,' said Detie quickly. Then she ran out of the room and Miss Rottenmeier ran after her.

'Do you want to be called Heidi or Adelheid?' asked Clara.

'Everyone calls me Heidi,' said the little girl.

'Well, I'll call you Heidi too,' said Clara. 'We'll be friends and you'll have lessons with my teacher, Mr Usher. You can learn to read while you are staying here.'

A few minutes later, Miss Rottenmeier came back into the study. She rang a bell, and Sebastian and Tinette entered.

'It's time for supper, Sebastian,' the housekeeper said. 'Tinette, go and prepare this girl's room.'

Sebastian pushed Clara's wheelchair into the dining-room. Then he lifted Clara up and put her onto a chair beside the table.

There was a roll of soft, white bread next to Heidi's plate. She remembered about the present for Grannie. She picked up the roll and put it in her pocket.

Miss Rottenmeier started talking. She told Heidi about her new life in the Sesemanns' house and told her how to behave. But Heidi was very tired after her long journey. Soon her eyes closed.

'Heidi's asleep,' said Clara, smiling.

So Miss Rottenmeier called the servants and they carried Heidi to her room.

———

The next morning, Heidi awoke and looked around her. She was in a high white bed, in a big strange room. Heidi ran to the windows and tried to look outside. But she was small and the windows were too high. She could not see out of them and she could not open them.

Miss Rottenmeier came into the room. 'Get dressed and come with me, Adelheid,' she said. 'It's time for breakfast.'

After breakfast, the girls went into the study and waited for Mr Usher, Clara's teacher.

'How can I open the windows in my room?' Heidi asked.

'Sebastian will open a window for you,' said Clara.

When Mr Usher arrived, Miss Rottenmeier took him into the dining-room and talked about Heidi.

'We have a problem,' she said. 'The child – Adelheid – is not a suitable companion for Miss Clara. Adelheid can't read so you won't be able to teach her any lessons. Clara's father must send her back home.'

'But perhaps she can *learn* to read,' said Mr Usher and he returned to the study.

Suddenly Miss Rottenmeier heard a loud crash from the study. She ran into the room and saw a terrible mess. There were books and papers all over the floor. The tablecloth was on the floor too, and an inkwell. Black ink was pouring out of the inkwell onto the carpet. Heidi had disappeared.

'Where is Adelheid?' asked Miss Rottenmeier. 'She must have done this.'

'It was an accident,' said Clara. 'Heidi ran out of the room and pulled the tablecloth down.'

Miss Rottenmeier went downstairs. Heidi was standing in the hall and the front door was open. The little girl was looking up and down the street.

'Why did you run away from your lessons?' asked Miss Rottenmeier.

'I heard the wind blowing through the fir trees,' replied Heidi. 'But I can't see the trees anywhere.'

Many carriages were passing along the street outside the house. Their wheels made a noise on the ground. It was like the sound of wind blowing in the branches of fir trees. This was the sound that Heidi heard.

'Fir trees!' said Miss Rottenmeier. 'Frankfurt isn't in the middle of a forest! You must sit still during your lessons, or I'll tie you to your chair!'

———

Each afternoon after dinner, Clara went to her room and rested. Heidi was left alone.

One afternoon, Heidi went to find Sebastian.

'Can you open a window, please?' she asked.

'Yes, of course,' he replied. He opened one of the tall windows in the sitting-room. But when Heidi looked out, she saw only streets and hundreds of houses.

'How can I see over the whole valley?' she asked.

'You must climb up a high building,' said Sebastian. 'A church tower might be tall enough.'

Heidi ran out of the front door and into the street. But she could not see any churches with tall towers. Then she saw a boy standing in the street. He was holding a hurdy-gurdy. As the boy turned the handle of the music box, he asked people for money.

'Can you take me to a church which has a high tower?' Heidi asked the boy.

'If you give me some money I'll take you,' he replied.

'I haven't got any money,' said Heidi. 'But my friend Clara has some. She'll give it to you.'

The boy took Heidi down a long street until they came to an old church with a high tower. But the church door was locked. Heidi saw a bell beside the door and rang it.

'I don't know the way home,' she said to the boy. 'Please will you wait for me and show me?'

'All right,' he said. 'But I'll want more money.'

After a few seconds, an old man opened the door. He was the keeper of the church tower.

'Can I climb up the tower?' asked Heidi.

'Yes,' said the old man. 'Come with me.'

He held Heidi's hand and they climbed up a great many steps. At last, they reached the top of the tower. But Heidi could not see any fir trees or mountains. She could only see the roofs, chimneys and towers of other buildings in the city and she felt sad.

Heidi and the old man began to go back down the steps. Halfway down the tower, they passed the keeper's room. The door was open and Heidi looked in. In the corner of the room, a large grey cat was sitting beside a basket. Inside the basket, there were eight little kittens.

'Oh, aren't they sweet!' cried Heidi, running into the room. She watched the kittens playing together.

'Would you like the kittens?' asked the keeper. 'You can have them if you want them.'

Heidi was very pleased. There was plenty of room for the kittens in Clara's big house.

'Where do you live?' asked the old man. 'I can bring them to you tomorrow.'

'I live at Mr Sesemann's house,' said Heidi. 'There's a dog's head made of gold on the front door.'

'I know that house,' said the keeper.

'Can I take two kittens now?' asked Heidi.

'Yes,' said the keeper. 'I'll bring the others tomorrow.'

Heidi smiled and picked up two kittens. She put the kittens into the pockets of her dress. Then the boy with the hurdy-gurdy took her back to the Sesemanns' house.

Heidi lifted the golden dog's head and knocked on the door. Sebastian opened it.

'Come in,' he said, when he saw Heidi. 'Miss Rottenmeier is angry with you.'

Sebastian shut the door quickly and did not notice the boy standing outside. He took Heidi into the dining-room. Miss Rottenmeier and Clara were sitting there.

'Adelheid,' said Miss Rottenmeier. 'Why did you run away?'

'*Miaou*,' said a kitten.

Miss Rottenmeier thought that it was Heidi's voice. She thought that Heidi was playing a joke.

'Don't speak to me in that silly voice!' she said.

'*Miaou, miaou, miaou!*' cried the kittens.

'Why are you making that noise?' asked Clara.

'It's not me, it's the kittens,' said Heidi.

'Kittens?! *Here?*' screamed the housekeeper. 'Sebastian! Come and take the horrible creatures away!' And she ran into the study and shut the door.

'Can you find a safe place for the kittens, Sebastian?' asked Clara.

'Yes, Miss Clara,' said Sebastian. 'I'll put the kittens in a basket. Then I'll take them to a room at the top of the house. They'll be safe there.'

Next morning, the boy with the hurdy-gurdy came to the front door. 'I want to see Clara,' he said to Sebastian. 'I showed her the way to a church tower yesterday. She said that she would give me some money.'

'You're telling lies,' said Sebastian. 'Miss Clara never goes out. She can't walk.'

'I saw her in the street,' said the boy. 'She's got short, curly, black hair and black eyes.'

'That's not Clara,' thought Sebastian. 'That's Heidi.'

Sebastian took the boy to the study. Clara and Heidi

were doing their lessons there. When Clara saw the hurdy-gurdy, she asked the boy to play some music.

But Miss Rottenmeier soon heard the sound of the hurdy-gurdy and ran into the room.

'Stop that noise at once!' she shouted.

Sebastian took the boy away and Clara and Heidi began their lessons again. Then Sebastian came back into the room. He was carrying a basket.

'A man has just brought this for Miss Clara,' he said.

Suddenly the lid of the basket opened, and six more kittens jumped out. They began to run around the room.

'The kittens are from the keeper of a church tower,' said Heidi.

'Oh, aren't they pretty!' said Clara.

'Sebastian! Catch the kittens and put them back in the basket,' said Miss Rottenmeier. She was very angry with Heidi.

'Miss Rottenmeier, please don't punish Heidi,' said Clara. 'My father is coming home in a few days. He'll decide what to do.'

The next few days passed quietly. Heidi tried to read, but it was very difficult. In the evenings, she told Clara about her life on the mountain. But this made Heidi feel very homesick[17]. She missed her home and the people there very much. She wanted to go back to the Alps.

At every meal, Heidi put a roll in her pocket for Grannie. Then she took the roll to her room and hid it in a cupboard.

One day, Miss Rottenmeier went into Heidi's room and saw Heidi's old hat on the table. She opened the door of Heidi's cupboard to put the hat inside. Suddenly, she saw a pile of rolls at the bottom of the cupboard. But the rolls were no longer soft and fresh – they were hard and dry.

'Why are you hiding these old rolls in your cupboard?' Miss Rottenmeier asked Heidi.

The housekeeper called Tinette. 'Go to Miss Adelheid's room,' she said. 'There is a pile of old rolls in the cupboard. Throw them away. And throw her old hat away too.'

'Oh, no!' cried Heidi, as tears fell from her eyes. 'I must keep my hat. And the rolls were for Grannie. Now she won't get any nice white bread.'

'Don't cry, Heidi,' said Clara. 'We can get more rolls for Grannie.'

Tinette took Heidi's hat away but Sebastian found it later and gave it back to her. She was very happy when she saw her old hat again. She hid it in her cupboard.

6

Clara's Grandmamma

Clara's father came home a few days later. Mr Sesemann had been away from Frankfurt on business. Immediately, he went to the study. As he greeted Clara and kissed her, he saw Heidi standing in the corner of the room.

'Ah! This is the little girl from Switzerland,' he said. 'Come and shake hands with me. Have you and Clara become good friends?'

'Oh, yes,' said Heidi. 'Clara is always kind to me.'

Later, Miss Rottenmeier spoke to Mr Sesemann about Heidi.

'I'm worried about the Swiss girl,' she said.

'I think that Clara likes her,' said Mr Sesemann.

'Yes,' said Miss Rottenmeier. 'But the child brings strange animals and people here. This isn't good for Miss Clara.'

Mr Sesemann went back to the study. He wanted to talk to Clara about Heidi so he turned to the little girl and spoke kindly to her.

'Heidi,' he said. 'Please will you go and fetch me a glass of fresh, cold water?'

Heidi went out and Mr Sesemann started to ask Clara questions. Clara told him about the kittens and the rolls. Mr Sesemann thought that these stories were very funny.

'Clara, do you want me to send Heidi home?' he asked.

'Oh, no, Papa!' said Clara. 'Since Heidi has come here, funny things happen every day.'

After many minutes, Heidi came back into the room. She was carrying a glass of water.

'Is the water cold?' asked Mr Sesemann.

'Oh, yes,' said Heidi. 'It's from a fountain in the street.

I had to walk a long way to find the fountain and I met a gentleman with white hair there. "Who asked you to fetch the water?" he asked me. "Mr Sesemann," I replied. Then the gentleman laughed and said, "Please give Mr Sesemann my best wishes."'

'What did this gentleman look like?' asked Mr Sesemann.

'He had a nice smile,' replied Heidi. 'And he had a stick with a handle in the shape of a horse's head.'

'That's Doctor Classen!' said Clara and her father together. The doctor and Mr Sesemann were good friends.

That evening, Mr Sesemann talked to Miss Rottenmeier.

'Heidi's going to stay here,' he said. 'Clara likes her very much. And soon, my mother is coming here for a visit. She'll help you with Heidi.'

Mr Sesemann stayed for two weeks. Then he had to go to Paris on business. The next day, a letter came from Mr Sesemann's mother.

'Grandmamma is coming tomorrow!' cried Clara happily. She loved her grandmother very much.

The next day, Mrs Sesemann arrived. While Clara talked to her grandmother, Heidi waited in her room. After about half an hour, Tinette came to fetch Heidi. She took her downstairs, to the study.

'Come here, my dear,' said Mrs Sesemann, when she saw Heidi. Her voice was kind and friendly.

Heidi loved Mrs Sesemann at once. She had pretty white hair and wore a cap[18] made of lace[19].

'What's your name?' asked Mrs Sesemann.

'Heidi. But people here call me Adelheid.'

'Then I shall call you Heidi, too,' said Mrs Sesemann. 'You may call me Grandmamma.'

The next afternoon, Clara went to her room to rest and

Mrs Sesemann called Heidi. She showed Heidi a big book with beautiful pictures. At first, Heidi looked at the pictures happily. But then suddenly, she started to cry.

There was one picture of a green field with animals. Light from the setting sun shone on the field.

'Perhaps Heidi thinks about her home when she looks at this picture,' thought Mrs Sesemann. 'Perhaps that is why she feels sad.'

'Don't cry, child,' said Mrs Sesemann kindly. 'I know a lovely story about this picture. But tell me – what have you learnt in your lessons?'

'Nothing, Grandmamma,' said Heidi. 'I can't read. It's too difficult.'

'Heidi,' said Mrs Sesemann, 'if you can learn to read, you can have this book.'

Heidi knew that she could not go home. She had to stay in Frankfurt. But every day, she felt more and more homesick. She missed Grandfather and her life on the mountains. She could not eat or sleep, and her face became pale. But Heidi did not want to tell the Sesemanns that she was homesick.

'Grandmamma and Clara have been very kind to me,' she thought. 'If they know that I'm unhappy, they'll be angry.'

But Mrs Sesemann could see that Heidi was sad. 'What's wrong, Heidi?' she asked. 'Why are you unhappy?'

'I can't tell you,' said Heidi sadly. 'I can't tell anyone.'

'Heidi,' said Grandmamma. 'If you have a problem or feel sad, you can ask God to help you.'

So Heidi told God all about her problems. 'Please, God,' she prayed[20]. 'Let me go home to my grandfather.'

One morning about a week later, Mr Usher spoke to Mrs Sesemann.

'Something wonderful has happened,' said the teacher. 'Heidi has learnt to read!'

That evening, Mrs Sesemann gave Heidi the book with the picture of the green fields and the animals.

'This book is yours now, Heidi,' she said.

From that time, Heidi liked reading very much. She sat with Mrs Sesemann every afternoon. She loved reading the stories aloud.

7

The Ghost

Every afternoon, Mrs Sesemann talked to Heidi. But she noticed that Heidi was still unhappy.

'My dear, why are you still sad?' asked Clara's grandmother. 'Is it the same problem? Did you tell God about it?'

'Yes,' said Heidi. 'But perhaps God didn't hear me, Grandmamma. I prayed every day, but nothing happened.'

'God always hears our prayers,' said Grandmamma. 'But He doesn't always answer them immediately.'

The next day, Mrs Sesemann returned to her home. Heidi and Clara were sad. The house was very quiet without Grandmamma. In the evening, Heidi came into the study, carrying a book.

'I'll read to you now, Clara,' she said.

Heidi started to read. But the story was about a grandmother who was dying. As she read, Heidi became very sad and started to cry.

'Perhaps Peter's Grannie will die,' she thought. 'Then I'll never see her again.'

Then Miss Rottenmeier came into the room.

'Adelheid, stop making that terrible noise,' she said. 'If you cry like that again, I'll take your book away.'

Heidi could not eat and she became very thin. At night, she lay in her bed and thought about home. Sometimes she went out in a carriage with Clara but everything in Frankfurt looked the same. There were lots of people and beautiful buildings but there was no grass, and there were no trees or mountains.

Autumn and winter passed, and then it was spring. Heidi became more and more homesick.

'Peter will be taking the goats onto the mountain, now,' she thought.

Strange things began to happen in the Sesemanns' house. One morning, when Sebastian came downstairs, he noticed that the front door was open.

'Who has opened the door?' he thought. 'Did a thief come into the house last night?'

Sebastian and a servant named John searched all through the house, but nothing had been stolen.

That evening, the servants carefully locked all the doors

and went to bed. But in the morning, the front door was open again. Sebastian told Miss Rottenmeier what had happened.

'You and John must stay near the hall tonight,' she said. 'Stay awake and watch the front door.'

That night, the wind blew strongly. Sebastian and John sat in a room beside the front door. They drank a bottle of wine and talked. But the sound of the wind made them sleepy, and soon they fell asleep. At midnight, they woke up again.

'I'll go and look at the front door,' said John. Then he took a lighted candle and went into the hall. Suddenly he ran back into the room again looking frightened.

'What's the matter?' asked Sebastian.

'The front door was open,' said John. 'And there was a figure[21] on the stairs. It was dressed in white clothes. It looked like a ghost!'

In the morning, John and Sebastian went to Miss Rottenmeier and told her what had happened. The housekeeper became frightened too. Immediately, she sent a letter to Mr Sesemann.

Please come quickly, she wrote. *We have a ghost in the house.* She received a reply the next day.

Miss Rottenmeier, said Mr Sesemann's letter. *I was very surprised by your story of the ghost. Are you sure that this ghost is real? I'm sorry, but I can't leave my business now.*

'Mr Sesemann doesn't believe me about the ghost,' thought Miss Rottenmeier. Then she had an idea. She went to Clara and told *her* about the ghost. Clara became very frightened.

'Oh, please write to Papa again!' Clara said. 'Ask him to come home.'

'Good,' thought the housekeeper. 'Mr Sesemann will be worried about Clara. He'll come home now.'

She sent another letter to Clara's father.

The ghost is still here, she wrote. *Clara is very frightened and upset. Please come home.*

Miss Rottenmeier's plan worked well. Two days later, Mr Sesemann came home. He went at once to Clara's room and found Miss Rottenmeier there.

'How is the "ghost"?' Mr Sesemann asked Miss Rottenmeier. He smiled as he spoke.

'It's not funny,' said the housekeeper. 'I'm sure that you won't laugh about it tomorrow.'

'I'm going to the dining-room. Please send Sebastian to me,' said Mr Sesemann.

Sebastian went into the dining-room and Mr Sesemann asked him to close the door.

'I want you to take a message to Doctor Classen,' he told the servant. 'Ask him to come here at nine o'clock tonight.'

Doctor Classen arrived after Clara and Heidi had gone to bed. This was the same doctor who had met Heidi at the fountain. Mr Sesemann told him about the ghost.

'Dear friend, let's catch this "ghost" tonight,' he said. 'I think that someone is playing a joke. Perhaps it's a friend of the servants. Or perhaps a thief is trying to steal something from the house. I've put two guns in the room beside the front door. If the "ghost" is a thief, we can frighten him with the guns.'

Mr Sesemann and Doctor Classen went to the room. Two guns, two glasses, and a bottle of wine were on a table. The men sat down in two comfortable chairs. They drank the wine and talked. The time passed quickly and soon it was after midnight.

Everything was quiet in the street outside. Then suddenly, they heard a noise in the hall. It was the sound of a key turning in the front door. Then they heard the door opening.

Each man picked up a gun and a lighted candle. They both ran into the hall. They saw that the front door was open. And a small figure, dressed in white, was standing beside it!

'Who's there?' shouted the doctor.

The figure turned round and gave a little cry. It was Heidi! She was wearing her night-clothes. She had no shoes on her feet. She was very surprised to see the two men.

'What are you doing here, child?' asked Mr Sesemann.

'I don't know,' said Heidi in a weak voice.

'I'll take her back to her room,' said the doctor. He put his gun on a table and held Heidi's hand. Then he led her upstairs to her bedroom.

'Don't be afraid Heidi,' said Doctor Classen kindly. 'Nothing bad is going to happen now.' He lifted the little girl and put her into the bed. Then he sat on a chair and held her hand. 'Tell me where you were going,' he said gently.

'Nowhere,' said Heidi. 'I didn't know that I was downstairs.'

'Were you dreaming?' asked the doctor.

'Yes,' replied Heidi. 'I have the same dream every night. I dream that I'm with Grandfather. I can hear the wind in the fir trees. I get up and open the door of our hut because I want to see the stars. But when I wake up, I'm still here in Frankfurt.'

Then Heidi started to cry.

'Go to sleep,' said the doctor quietly. 'In the morning, everything will be all right.'

He left the room and went to find Mr Sesemann.

'Heidi is walking in her sleep,' said the doctor. 'She's dreaming about her home. Every night, while she's sleeping, she opens the front door. She thinks that she's at home in her grandfather's hut. Heidi's very homesick, she's become very thin and ill. You must send her home. If you don't send her back to the mountains now, it may be too late. Perhaps she will never become well, or happy, again.'

Mr Sesemann was worried when he heard this news.

'Then Heidi must go home tomorrow,' he said.

8

Home Again

At breakfast the next morning, Mr Sesemann spoke to Heidi.

'Heidi, I've some good news for you,' he said. 'You're going home today.'

'Home!' said Heidi. Then she smiled with joy.

'Yes,' said Mr Sesemann. 'We'll pack a case with your things and Sebastian will go with you. You'll travel to Basle today. Then tomorrow, you'll go to Mayenfeld by train. I'll write a letter to your grandfather.'

Clara was very upset that Heidi was leaving. Mr Sesemann went to his daughter's room and talked to her.

'Heidi's very homesick Clara,' he said. 'She walks in her sleep at night because she's so unhappy. She is becoming ill. She must go home.'

Sebastian took Heidi's case to Clara's room. Clara put some pretty dresses and other things for Heidi into it. There was also a basket with twelve fresh rolls for Grannie. Heidi fetched her old hat and her book with pictures. She put the book and the hat into the basket. Then she put on a pretty new hat and went downstairs.

The Sesemanns' carriage was waiting outside. Clara and Heidi kissed each other and said goodbye.

When Heidi got into the carriage, Sebastian got in too.

'Goodbye, Heidi,' said Mr Sesemann. 'Clara and I will often think of you. I hope that you have a good journey.'

'Thank you for everything,' said Heidi. 'And please thank the doctor too.'

The next day, Sebastian and Heidi arrived at Mayenfeld.

Outside the railway station, there was a man with a small cart pulled by a horse.

'Can you tell me the way to Dörfli?' asked Sebastian.

'I'm going to Dörfli myself,' said the man. 'I'm the baker in the village. If the case isn't heavy, I can take it on my cart. I can take the child too.'

'Thank you very much,' said Sebastian. He gave Heidi Mr Sesemann's letter and a packet.

'This is a present for you from Mr Sesemann,' he told her. 'And the letter is for your grandfather. Goodbye, Heidi.'

The baker took Heidi to Dörfli on his cart. The villagers were very surprised when they saw Heidi and wanted to ask her lots of questions. But she did not want to stop.

'Thank you,' she said to the baker. 'I'll carry the basket. Grandfather will fetch my case tomorrow.' Then she started to run up the mountain.

'Will Grannie still be there?' she thought. 'Oh, I hope that she isn't dead.'

When she came to Peter's hut, Heidi opened the door and ran inside.

'Who's there?' said a voice from the corner of the room.

'It's Heidi, Grannie!' cried Heidi. Then she threw her arms round the old woman's neck and held her tightly.

'Yes, that's Heidi's voice,' said Grannie. She moved her hands over Heidi's head and began to cry. 'Oh! And this is Heidi's curly hair.'

'Yes, Grannie, it's really me. Don't cry,' said Heidi. 'I'm here and I'll never go away again. I'll come and see you every day. And I've brought you some lovely rolls.' She took the rolls from her basket and put them on Grannie's knees.

'What a lovely present!' said Grannie. 'But *you* are the best present.'

Then Bridget came in. She was surprised and pleased to see Heidi too. 'You're wearing a pretty hat,' she said.

'You can have it,' said Heidi. 'I don't want it any more.' She took off the hat and gave it to Bridget.

Heidi put on her old hat. 'I'll come and see you again tomorrow,' she said to Grannie. Then she went on up the mountain.

The sun was setting. Its light shone on the mountains and made them the colour of bright red flames. Soon, the sun had almost disappeared and the sky began to get dark. At last, she saw the tops of the three old fir trees. Then she saw the hut. And there was Grandfather! He was sitting on the bench, smoking his pipe. Heidi dropped her basket and ran towards him.

'Grandfather!' she cried. Then she threw her arms round his neck.

The old man was very surprised and pleased.

'Why have you come back, Heidi?' he asked. 'Did the family in Frankfurt send you away?'

'Oh, no, Grandfather. Clara and her family were very kind to me. But I was homesick, so Mr Sesemann sent me home. I've got a letter for you, I'm sure that it'll tell you everything.'

Then Heidi gave him the letter and the packet. The old man read the letter carefully.

'The letter says that the packet is for you, Heidi,' he said. 'There's money in it. You must buy a bed and any clothes that you need.'

'I don't want the money,' said Heidi happily. 'I've got a bed already, and Clara gave me lots of clothes.'

They went inside the hut. Heidi sat on her own chair and her grandfather gave her a mug of milk. It tasted delicious.

Suddenly they heard a whistle outside. It was Peter and the goats.

'Hello, Peter!' called Heidi, running towards him. 'Hello, Daisy and Dusky. Do you remember me?'

All the goats came towards Heidi. As she greeted each goat, she put her arms round its neck.

That night, Heidi slept very well. She was very happy to be home again. She dreamt about the sun on the mountains, and the wind in the fir trees.

The next day, Grandfather went down to Dörfli to fetch Heidi's case while Heidi went to visit Grannie.

'Did you like the rolls, Grannie?' she asked.

'Yes!' said Grannie. 'They were delicious.'

Then Heidi had an idea.

'I've lots of money now, Grannie,' she said. 'I can buy rolls from the baker in Dörfli. You can have a fresh roll every day.'

Then she saw some books on the shelf. 'And I can read now,' she said. 'Shall I read a story from this book to you?'

Heidi took the book from the shelf and sat down. She opened it and began to read. Grannie was very pleased as she listened.

The next day was Sunday. It was a beautiful day and the sun shone on Heidi's face as she lay in her bed. She heard the birds singing in the fir trees. She heard the sound of church bells ringing, far down in the valley.

'Heidi!' called Grandfather. 'Put on your best dress. We'll go down to the village together.'

Heidi quickly put on one of her dresses from Frankfurt and climbed down the ladder. When she saw her grandfather, she stopped. She was very surprised. He was wearing a jacket with silver buttons.

'You look very handsome, Grandfather,' she said.

'And you look very pretty,' he replied.

He held her hand as they walked down the mountain together. When they reached Dörfli, Grandfather took Heidi to the pastor's house. The pastor was happy to see them.

'I want to return to the village,' said Grandfather.

49

'You were right and I was wrong, pastor. Winters on the mountain are too cold for Heidi. I'll come back to Dörfli during winter.'

When Heidi and Grandfather left the pastor's house, the villagers were waiting for them. They had heard about Heidi and Uncle Alp's visit. Everyone wanted to say hello to them.

At last, the little girl and her grandfather left Dörfli and climbed up the mountain to Peter's hut.

'Hello, Grannie!' called Uncle Alp. 'I can see that your hut needs some repairs. I'll do the work before the winter comes.'

'Is that you, Uncle Alp?' said the blind woman. 'This is a lovely surprise!'

'Heidi's with me,' said the old man. 'She's returned to our mountain.'

'Please don't let her go away again,' said Grannie.

At that moment, Peter came in. He brought a letter for Heidi from the post office in Dörfli. The letter was from Clara. Heidi read it aloud while everyone listened.

Dear Heidi,

It has been very quiet here, since you went away. I miss you very much. But Papa says that I can come and visit you and your grandfather in the autumn. Grandmamma will come with us. We would like to visit Peter's Grannie too.

Your friend, Clara

When Heidi and Grandfather left the pastor's house,
the villagers were waiting for them.

9

A Visitor from Frankfurt

Clara was sad that Heidi had returned to the mountains. She missed her friend and companion very much. So Mr Sesemann told Clara that she could visit Heidi in the autumn. But that summer, Clara became very ill. By September she was better, but she was still not very strong. Doctor Classen was worried about her.

'Clara isn't well enough to visit Heidi yet,' he told Mr Sesemann. 'The weather in the mountains may be cold now and Clara won't be able to stay in the hut with Heidi. Wait until next May. The weather will be warmer then. Let Clara visit Heidi in May.'

As he spoke, Doctor Classen looked very sad. He was remembering his own daughter. She had died a few months earlier. Now the doctor had no family. He was all alone.

Mr Sesemann saw that the doctor was unhappy. 'I have an idea,' he said. 'Clara can't go to Switzerland now, but *you* can go. You can visit Heidi for us.'

The doctor was very surprised. But before he could reply, Mr Sesemann took him to see Clara. At first, Clara was disappointed and sad because she could not visit Heidi. But when she heard about her father's plan she was happy.

'Oh, Doctor Classen!' said Clara, 'Please go to Switzerland and see Heidi for me. You can take some presents to Heidi and Grannie.'

Clara prepared the presents and Miss Rottenmeier packed them in a large box. First, there was a thick coat with a warm hood for Heidi. Next, there was a warm shawl and a box of cakes for Grannie. There was tobacco for Heidi's grandfather, and sausage for Peter, his mother and Grannie.

When all these things were packed, Sebastian took the box to the doctor's house.

——

A few days later, Heidi was outside the hut. She was listening to the wind in the fir trees when suddenly she saw the doctor coming up the mountain. Heidi ran down the path and greeted him excitedly.

'Doctor Classen!' she cried. Then she stopped and looked down the mountain. 'But where are Clara and Grandmamma?'

'I'm sorry, Heidi,' said the doctor. 'I've come alone. I'm afraid Clara's been ill. She cannot travel now. But she'll come with her grandmother, in the spring.'

'Oh,' said Heidi sadly. She was very disappointed. Then she looked at the doctor and saw that he looked sad. She wanted him to feel happy again.

'Well,' she said. 'It'll soon be spring. Come and see Grandfather.'

Heidi held the doctor's hand and led him towards the hut. She had talked a lot about the doctor to her grandfather. Uncle Alp greeted Doctor Classen warmly.

'I hope that you'll spend these beautiful autumn days with us,' said Grandfather. 'I'm sorry, but you can't stay here in the evenings. There isn't a bed for you to sleep in. But there's a good hotel in Dörfli. Come and visit us every day. I'll show you the mountain.'

'Thank you,' said the doctor, smiling.

At midday, Grandfather brought the table out of the hut.

'Please eat with us, doctor,' he said. 'Our food is simple, but our dining-room has a wonderful view.'

'Yes, it does!' said the doctor. He looked down to the valley. Bright sunshine was shining into it.

Heidi brought milk, bread, toasted cheese and meat to

the table. The doctor enjoyed his meal very much.

'Clara must come here,' Doctor Classen thought. 'She'll feel better when she's in the mountains.'

After the meal, they saw a man walking up the mountain path with a huge parcel on his back.

'There are some presents from Frankfurt in the parcel,' said the doctor.

Heidi was very excited when she saw all the lovely things inside the parcel. Uncle Alp was very pleased with the tobacco.

As the sun was setting, the doctor began his journey back to Dörfli. They all walked down the mountain together, as far as Peter's home. The doctor held Heidi's hand, and Grandfather carried the presents.

'Doctor, would you like to go up to the pasture with the goats tomorrow?' Heidi asked.

'Yes,' he replied. 'Let's go together.'

The doctor and Grandfather went on to Dörfli, and Heidi ran into Peter's hut.

Grannie and Bridget were very pleased with their presents. When Peter saw the sausage, he smiled happily. It was the best sausage that he had ever seen.

'Clara and her grandmother are very kind,' said Grannie. 'This wonderful shawl will be warm in the winter.'

The next day, Doctor Classen went with Heidi, Peter, and the goats, to the pasture. Before they left the hut, Uncle Alp gave Peter a bag of food. There was a large piece of meat for the doctor's lunch.

When they reached the pasture, the children and the doctor sat down. The goats moved about, eating the fresh grass. Far above the mountainside, a hawk flew in large circles in the sky.

'It's very beautiful here, Heidi,' said the doctor. 'You can see the sky, mountains and trees. You have sunshine, fresh air and good food. You didn't have these things in Frankfurt. That's why you became ill.' Then he remembered his daughter and became sad again.

Heidi was very pleased that the doctor had come up to the pasture. But Peter was not happy because Heidi talked to the doctor, and not to him.

At midday, the boy opened the bag of food.

'I'm not hungry,' said the doctor. 'I only want a little milk. I'd like to walk further up the mountain.'

'You only want milk?' said Peter in surprise. 'What about all the food in the bag?'

'*You* can have my food,' replied the doctor.

Peter was pleased. He began to like the doctor.

———

All that month, the weather was fine. Doctor Classen walked from Dörfli to the hut every morning. He went for long walks with Grandfather. The old man told him many interesting things about life in the mountains.

At last the doctor's holiday ended. It was time for him to return to Frankfurt.

'I wish that I could take you with me, Heidi,' he said.

Heidi thought about Frankfurt, with its tall houses and streets full of people. Then she remembered Miss Rottenmeier, who was unkind to her.

'Yes,' she said, 'but it would be nicer if *you* came back here.'

'Heidi,' said the doctor. 'If I ever feel ill or lonely, will you come and see me?'

'Oh, yes,' said Heidi. 'I love you almost as much as Grandfather!'

So the doctor felt very happy when he left. 'This is a wonderful place!' he thought.

10

Winter in Dörfli

Grandfather promised to take Heidi down to Dörfli for the winter. In the middle of October, the weather became colder. So he took Heidi and the goats down to his house in the village.

The house was near the church in Dörfli. In the past, Uncle Alp had lived there with his son, Tobias. The old man had to make many repairs to the house because it had been empty for many years. All through the autumn, Uncle Alp worked very hard.

Heidi liked her new home very much. Her room had pictures on the walls and a warm stove. One day, Grandfather brought her bed of hay from the hut and put it in her new room. In the afternoon, snow began to fall.

Four days later, Heidi went to her grandfather.

'I must go and see Grannie today,' she said.

'No, Heidi,' he said. 'You can't go up the mountain today, or tomorrow. The snow is deep and more snow is falling. Wait until the snow freezes and becomes hard. Then you can walk over it easily.'

A few days later, the snow froze and Peter came to the house in Dörfli. Heidi went up the mountain with him. But when they arrived at Peter's hut, Grannie was not sitting in the corner of the room.

'Grannie's in bed,' said Bridget. 'She isn't very well.'

Heidi ran quickly into Grannie's room. The shawl from Frankfurt was round the old woman's shoulders.

'Are you ill, Grannie?' asked Heidi.

'No, no,' said the old woman. 'I'm cold and my bed isn't very comfortable. But I'll be better soon. I have lovely rolls every day. I have this fine warm shawl, and now you're here. Will you read to me?'

Heidi fetched a book and started to read aloud. Soon there was a happy smile on Grannie's face.

It began to get dark outside. 'I have to go now, Grannie,' said Heidi.

She said goodnight and went outside with Peter. The moon was shining on the snow. Peter fetched his sledge and he got onto it with Heidi. They travelled down to Dörfli very quickly.

Heidi could not sleep that night. 'When I read to Grannie, she's happy. But I can't visit her every day, because of the snow,' she thought.

Suddenly Heidi had an idea. 'I know what to do,' she thought, 'I must talk to Peter.' Then she closed her eyes and slept well until morning.

Heidi fetched a book and started to read aloud.
Soon there was a happy smile on Grannie's face.

Heidi went to school every day in Dörfli and worked hard at her lessons. Sometimes Peter went to school too. But usually he stayed away. The lessons were difficult for him.

When Heidi saw Peter again, she ran towards him.

'I've had an idea,' she said excitedly. 'I know how we can help Grannie! You must learn to read!'

'I can't,' said Peter. 'It's too difficult.'

'No, it isn't,' said Heidi. 'I'll teach you. Then you can read to Grannie every day.'

So Heidi began to teach Peter. Every day, she taught him some more letters of the alphabet. And he went to school every day too. Then more snow fell. Soft, thick snow covered everything and Heidi could not go up the mountain to visit Grannie.

One evening, three weeks later, Peter had a surprise for his mother.

'I can read now,' he said.

'What did you say?' replied Bridget.

'I can read now,' he repeated. 'Grannie, shall I read you a story? Heidi told me to do that.'

Bridget fetched a book and Peter sat down at the table. He began to read aloud. Both Grannie and Bridget were very surprised and pleased.

At school the next day, there was a reading lesson.

'Try to read a little,' said the teacher to Peter.

Peter read aloud from his book.

The teacher was shocked. 'Peter! You can read now!' he said. 'You made no mistakes. Who helped you?'

'It was Heidi,' replied Peter.

After this, Peter often read for Grannie. But when a word was too difficult for him, he did not read it.

'Peter tries hard,' Grannie told Bridget. 'But he doesn't read as well as Heidi. He misses lots of words. I'll be pleased when it is spring. Then Heidi will visit me again!'

11

More Visitors for Heidi

The long winter passed. It was now May. The snow had disappeared, and the slopes of the mountains were covered in fresh green grass and flowers. Heidi and Uncle Alp returned to their hut.

One day, Peter brought a letter for Heidi. It had arrived at the post office in Dörfli. The letter was from Clara.

Dear Heidi, it said. I am coming to Switzerland to visit you very soon. Grandmamma is coming with me. I want to see you again very much and I want to meet Peter and the goats.

Your friend, Clara

Heidi was very pleased with this news. But Peter was not happy. He did not want any visitors from Frankfurt on the mountain.

One morning in June, Heidi saw two men coming to the hut. They were carrying a chair on two poles. A girl was sitting in the chair and beside her, a lady was riding on a horse. Two other men followed behind. One man was pushing an empty wheelchair, the other man was carrying a large bundle on his back.

'Grandfather! Come and look!' shouted Heidi. 'Clara and Grandmamma have come!' And she ran to welcome Clara.

Mrs Sesemann got down from her horse and Heidi greeted her happily.

Then Uncle Alp came and greeted Mrs Sesemann warmly.

They were carrying a chair on two poles.

'What a beautiful place!' said Clara, looking round at the high mountains and the fir trees.

'Let me carry you to your chair,' said Uncle Alp to Clara. He lifted her and put her gently into the wheelchair.

'Oh, Heidi,' said Clara. 'I wish that I could run about like you.'

Uncle Alp brought the table and chairs out of the hut. He put some milk and cheese on the table, and everyone sat down to dinner.

'Your dining-room has a wonderful view,' said Mrs Sesemann. 'I've never enjoyed a meal so much.'

'Yes,' said Clara, 'and the food tastes wonderful.'

Later, Heidi took Mrs Sesemann to the loft.

'Here is my bed,' said Heidi. 'It's made of hay.'

Uncle Alp carried Clara up the ladder, so that she could see Heidi's bedroom too.

'This is a lovely place to sleep!' said Clara.

'I have an idea,' Uncle Alp said to Mrs Sesemann. 'Let Clara stay here with us for a time. I'm sure that she'll get stronger. I'll make a comfortable bed for her in the loft. Then she can be with Heidi.'

When they heard this, both girls were very happy. Mrs Sesemann agreed to the plan.

There were some warm rugs in Clara's bundle. Uncle Alp carried the rugs up to the loft and made a bed for her.

In the afternoon, Mrs Sesemann got on her horse and Uncle Alp took her down the mountain. She was going to stay in Dörfli but she promised to visit again soon.

At sunset, Peter arrived with the goats. Heidi called each one so that Clara could learn its name. Clara met Snowflake and Spot, Finch and Daisy, Dusky and Big Turk.

The next morning, Heidi helped Clara to get dressed. When the girls were ready, Uncle Alp lifted Clara and carried her down the ladder. He put Clara into her wheelchair and pushed the chair outside so that Clara could breathe the fresh mountain air.

'I wish that I could stay here for ever,' she said. She felt the warm sunshine on her face and hands.

Uncle Alp brought two mugs of goat's milk out of the hut and gave a mug to each girl.

'Drink this!' he said to Clara. 'It's milk from Daisy. It'll make you strong.'

Clara had never drunk goat's milk before. She liked it very much.

'What shall we do now, Heidi?' she asked.

'Let's write letters to Grandmamma,' said Heidi. 'Perhaps she's worried about you up here.'

'All right,' said Clara, 'but please can we stay outside? It's wonderful to be outdoors.'

The day passed quickly. At dinner time, Uncle Alp gave the girls more delicious food. Later, Peter brought the goats down from the pasture. The girls called 'Goodnight!' to him but he did not reply. He went on, down the mountain.

The next day, two men arrived from Dörfli. They were carrying the parts of two beds on their backs. The men had also brought a letter from Mrs Sesemann which explained that the beds were for Clara and Heidi. Uncle Alp helped the men to build the beds in the loft.

———

Clara began to grow stronger. The girls wrote to Grandmamma every day, so Mrs Sesemann knew that Clara was enjoying her time on the mountain.

Uncle Alp liked Clara very much. But he was sad that she had to sit in a wheelchair all the time. He wanted Clara to try and walk. Each morning, when he put her into the wheelchair, he spoke to her gently.

'Can you try and stand by yourself for a short time?' he asked.

Clara tried to stand, but her legs were weak and painful. She soon sat down again.

―――

It was a beautiful summer. The sun shone brightly and pretty flowers covered the ground.

'Grandfather, please will you take us up to the pasture tomorrow?' asked Heidi, one day.

'Yes,' replied Uncle Alp.

When Peter arrived, Heidi told him the news.

'We're coming up the mountain with you tomorrow,' she said excitedly. 'We're going to spend the whole day on the pasture!'

Peter said nothing. He did not want Clara to come up to the pasture. He only wanted to spend time with his friend, Heidi.

12

A Wonderful Surprise

Uncle Alp got up early the next morning. First, he fetched Clara's wheelchair and put it outside the hut. Then he went inside to wake Clara and Heidi.

When Peter arrived, he saw the wheelchair outside the hut. He thought about Clara and became very angry.

'Heidi used to come up to the pasture with me every day,' he thought. 'But now Clara's here Heidi doesn't spend any time with me. She's always with Clara.'

Suddenly, Peter ran towards the wheelchair and pushed it. The chair moved down the slope, faster and faster until it fell over the ledge and crashed onto the rocks far below.

'Good!' thought Peter. 'Clara won't be able to go anywhere without her wheelchair. She'll have to leave.'

Then he ran up to the pasture as fast as he could.

Uncle Alp came out of the hut carrying Clara in his arms. Heidi was following them.

'Where's Clara's chair?' asked Uncle Alp.

'I don't know,' said Heidi. 'Perhaps the wind blew it off the mountain.'

Uncle Alp put Clara onto the bench. Then he walked to the ledge and looked down the mountainside. He saw the wheelchair far below. It was broken into pieces.

'That's strange,' he thought. 'How did the wheelchair get down there? I don't believe that the wind did this. Did someone push the chair down the mountain?'

Clara was very upset when Uncle Alp told her about the chair. 'Oh!' she said. 'Now we can't go up to the pasture.'

'Yes, we can,' said Uncle Alp. 'Where's Peter? He's very late today.'

After breakfast, Uncle Alp carried Clara up the mountain path and Heidi followed with Daisy and Dusky. When they arrived at the pasture, they saw Peter with the other goats.

'Have you seen Clara's wheelchair?' asked Uncle Alp.

'No,' said Peter.

Uncle Alp looked at Peter but he did not say anything more. 'Peter often looks angrily at Clara,' he thought. 'He's jealous because Heidi spends all her time with Clara. Perhaps Peter pushed the chair off the mountain.'

Uncle Alp put Clara down on the warm, soft grass.

'I'll come back for you later,' he said. 'But now I must go down and find your wheelchair.'

It was a lovely, sunny day. The two girls sat and talked happily together. Sometimes Snowflake, the little white goat, came and sat beside them.

65

'May I leave you alone for a few minutes, Clara?' asked Heidi. 'I want to go and see the flowers.'

'Yes, of course,' said Clara. 'I'm happy here, with Snowflake.'

Heidi ran further up the path and looked at the flowers. They were very beautiful. She wanted Clara to see them too so she ran back to her friend.

'You must come and see the flowers,' she said. 'Perhaps I can carry you.'

'You can't carry me,' said Clara. 'You're too small.'

Then Heidi had an idea.

'Peter!' she called. 'I want you to do something. Come here!'

'No,' said Peter, 'I don't want to.'

'If you don't come immediately,' said Heidi angrily, 'I'll do something that you won't like.'

Now Peter was afraid. Did Heidi know that *he* had pushed Clara's chair off the mountain? Was she going to tell Uncle Alp? Peter went over to Heidi.

'What do you want?' he asked.

'Stand on the left side of Clara,' said Heidi. 'I'll stand on her right side. We can both help her to stand.'

Peter did what Heidi asked. Now Clara was standing up.

'Put your arm round my neck, Clara,' said Heidi. 'Peter, hold Clara's other arm. Now, Clara, try and walk a little. Go slowly! Don't be afraid. Peter and I are holding you.'

Clara moved one foot, then the other.

'Oh, that hurts!' she said. But she tried again. And very slowly, she began to move forward. 'Oh, Heidi!' she cried. 'Look at me! Look at me! I'm walking!'

Clara was really walking. Each time that she took a step, she was getting stronger.

'This is wonderful, Clara!' said Heidi excitedly. 'Soon you won't need your wheelchair any more!'

Heidi and Peter took Clara further up the path, and they sat down together on the grass. Clara looked at the beautiful flowers.

'I can really walk!' she thought happily.

Heidi and Peter helped Clara to walk back to the pasture. Then they had dinner and the girls gave Peter some of their food, so he was very happy. But when Peter remembered Clara's wheelchair, he stopped enjoying the food.

Uncle Alp arrived and when Heidi told him the exciting news about Clara, he was very pleased. He helped Clara to stand and walk a few steps. He saw that the news was true. Clara was able to walk again.

In the evening, Peter took the goats back down to Dörfli and he got a shock. The villagers were staring at something on the ground. It was the broken pieces of Clara's wheelchair.

'But how did the chair fall off the mountain?' asked the schoolteacher. 'That chair was very expensive. The girl's father will be very angry.'

Peter became frightened. 'Perhaps Mr Sesemann will send a policeman from Frankfurt,' he thought. 'The policeman will find out that I pushed the chair off the mountain.'

The next morning, Heidi and Clara wrote to Mrs Sesemann. But they did not tell her that Clara could walk. They wanted to give her a surprise. So they asked her to come to the mountain in one week's time.

The next few days passed happily. Every day, Clara grew stronger. Every day, she walked a little further. After seven days had passed, Mrs Sesemann arrived. As she came up the path, she saw Clara and Heidi sitting outside the hut.

'You look well, Clara,' she said. 'But where's your chair?'

Heidi stood up, and then Clara stood up too. She held Heidi's arm and began to walk slowly towards her grandmother. Clara was walking! Mrs Sesemann was so surprised and happy that she began to cry.

Uncle Alp came out of the house.

'You've helped Clara to walk again!' Mrs Sesemann said. 'And she looks so healthy and happy! How can our family thank you? I'll write to Clara's father and tell him the wonderful news.'

But Clara's father had a surprise for them. He was already in Switzerland and was coming to visit Clara. At that moment, he was walking up from Dörfli. But he was hot and tired and he could not find the right path. He stopped to rest for a few moments.

Suddenly, he saw a boy coming down the mountain. It was Peter.

'I'm looking for a man called Uncle Alp,' said Mr Sesemann. 'Do you know this man? He lives on the mountain with a child called Heidi. Some people from Frankfurt are visiting them.'

'This is a policeman from Frankfurt!' thought Peter. 'He's looking for me. He's going to ask me questions about the wheelchair!' And Peter ran away as fast as he could.

'What a strange boy!' thought Mr Sesemann as he walked further up the mountain. At last, he saw Uncle Alp's hut and the three fir trees.

When Heidi and Clara saw Mr Sesemann, they shouted with joy. Immediately, they began to walk down the path towards him.

Mr Sesemann stared at his daughter. He could not speak because he was so shocked. Then he held Clara tightly in his arms and tears fell from his eyes.

'Is this really happening?' he asked. 'Clara, you are *walking*! This is such a wonderful surprise!'

When Mr Sesemann met Uncle Alp, they greeted each other like old friends. Mr Sesemann thanked Heidi's grandfather for everything that he had done for Clara.

Later, Mrs Sesemann saw Peter near the fir trees.

When Heidi and Clara saw Mr Sesemann, they shouted with joy.

'What's wrong with that boy?' she asked Uncle Alp. 'Why is he hiding in the trees? Is he afraid of us?'

'That boy is the "wind" which blew Clara's wheelchair off the mountain,' said Uncle Alp. 'His name is Peter. He became jealous when Heidi spent all her time with Clara.'

Mrs Sesemann called Peter's name and the boy came towards her. He was very worried.

'I know what you did and why you did it,' she said kindly. 'But you didn't make trouble for Clara, you helped her. When she didn't have her chair, she learnt to walk again. I want to give you a present, Peter. What would you like?'

'A present!' said Peter. 'Well, I'd like a penny.'

'All right,' said Mrs Sesemann, laughing. 'You can certainly have a penny. You can have one penny every week, for the rest of your life.'

Peter was very happy. 'I'm not in trouble after all!' he thought. And he ran up the mountain as fast as he could.

Mrs Sesemann turned to Uncle Alp.

'Dear friend,' she said. 'You've done so much for Clara. What can we do for you? Is there anything that you need?'

'I want only one thing,' said Uncle Alp. 'I'm an old man. What will happen to Heidi when I die? Please, will you look after her?'

'Yes, of course,' said Mr Sesemann. 'We love Heidi very much. We'll always take care of her.'

'Heidi,' asked Mrs Sesemann. 'Is there anything that *you* want?'

'Yes,' replied Heidi. 'My bed in Frankfurt is warm and comfortable. I'd like to give it to Grannie. Then she'll be able to sleep well every night.'

'I'll write to Miss Rottenmeier at once,' said Mr Sesemann. 'I'll ask her to send the bed to Grannie.'

'I'll tell Grannie at once!' said Heidi excitedly.

'Let's all go down to Grannie's house and tell her,' said Mrs Sesemann.

But when Grannie heard this news, she did not look happy.

'That's very kind,' she said sadly, 'but are the Sesemanns taking you back to Frankfurt, Heidi? I think that I'll die without you.'

'No, no,' said Mrs Sesemann. 'Heidi's not coming to Frankfurt. She's going to stay here on the mountain. We'll come and visit her again next year.'

The next morning, the Sesemanns prepared to leave the mountain. When Heidi and Clara said goodbye to each other, Clara began to cry.

'Don't be sad, Clara,' said Heidi. 'Summer will soon be here again. Then you'll come back to visit us.'

'Yes,' said Clara. 'I'm going to miss you very much, Heidi. But I'll think about next year. We'll have wonderful times together on the mountain!'

Points for Understanding

1

1 Where is Detie taking Heidi? Why?
2 Who is Peter and what work does he do?
3 Describe Uncle Alp's hut.

2

Who are Snowflake and Finch? What happens to Finch?

3

1 Soft, thick snow covered the mountain.
   (a) After this snowfall, what happened to: (i) Peter (ii) the goats (iii) Uncle Alp and Heidi?
   (b) Then the snow froze and became hard. What did Uncle Alp and Heidi do?
2 Heidi became upset. (a) Why? (b) How did Uncle Alp help?

4

1 Who came to take Heidi to Frankfurt? Why?
2 How did Uncle Alp change after Heidi left?

5

1 Describe the people in the Sesemann house.
2 Why did Heidi (a) run into the street? (b) climb to the top of the church tower?
3 Which people and things came to the house because of Heidi?

6

1 Who did Heidi meet at the fountain?
2 What made Heidi homesick? Why could she not tell Mrs Sesemann about it?
3 How are a book and reading important in this chapter?

7

1 Why did Clara's father come home?
2 (a) What happened every night? (b) Who did this?
   (c) Who found out the truth? (d) Why did this thing happen?
   (e) What happened next?

8

1 How did Heidi feel about Mr Sesemann's news?
2 What did Heidi take with her to Switzerland?
3 Describe Uncle Alp and Heidi's visit to Dörfli.

9

1 Clara sends some presents to Switzerland. (a) What were they? (b) Who brought them? (c) Why did Clara not bring them herself?
2 How did these people feel about the visitor? (a) Heidi (b) Uncle Alp (c) Peter.

10

Heidi had an idea. What was it? Who did it help?

11

1 Describe Clara's first morning on the mountain.
2 What did Uncle Alp make Clara do every morning?

12

1 Why did Peter push Clara's wheelchair off the mountain?
   What happened to Clara after this?
2 Which presents or promises did these people give or receive?
   (a) Peter (b) Heidi (c) Uncle Alp (d) Grannie
   (e) Grandmamma (f) Mr Sesemann.

Glossary

1 **injured** – *to injure* (page 4)
to be hurt in an accident or an attack.
2 **heroine** (page 5)
the main female character of a book, film, or play.
3 **stockings** (page 9)
a piece of clothing that is worn on a woman's foot and leg.
4 **scarf** (page 9)
a piece of cloth that you wear round your neck or head.
5 **steep** (page 11)
a steep slope goes up or down very quickly.
6 **branch** (page 12)
one of the parts of a tree that grows out of its trunk (main stem).
7 **sack** (page 14)
a large strong bag for storing and carrying things.
8 **whistle** (page 15)
to make a high sound by forcing air through your lips.
9 **removing** – *to remove* (page 21)
to take someone or something away from a place.
10 **repairing** – *to repair* (page 22)
to fix something that is broken or damaged.
11 **shutters** (page 22)
a cover that can be closed over the outside of a window.
12 **blind** (page 23)
unable to see.
13 **pastor** (page 26)
a priest in some Christian churches.
14 **invalid** (page 26)
someone who is ill or injured and cannot look after themselves.
Clara cannot walk and sits in a *wheelchair*.
15 **rolls** (page 28)
bread in the form of a small round shape.
16 **companion** (page 29)
someone who is with you or who you spend a lot of time with.
17 **homesick** (page 36)
feeling sad and alone because you are far from home.
18 **cap** (page 38)
a soft hat.

19 **lace** (page 38)

a light delicate cloth with patterns of small holes in it.

20 **pray** (page 40)

to speak to God, usually to give thanks or to ask for help.

21 **figure** (page 42)

a person, or the shape of a person.

Exercises

Vocabulary: words in the story

Put words from the box into the correct sentences. There are two extra words.

> shutters   whistle   branches   blind   repairing   invalid   steep
> homesick   rolls   scarf   injured   companion   wheelchair
> removing   lessons   disappeared   figure

1 Many soldiers were .... in the war.

2 The mountain slopes are .... and the paths are dangerous.

3 A long red .... was tied tightly around her body.

4 Three old fir trees, with big .... grew next to the hut.

5 Grannie could not see. She had been .... for many years.

6 A woman was .... a jacket with a needle and thread.

7 Grandfather worked hard for several hours .... the snow from the walls of the hut with a large shovel.

8 Clara is an .... She can't walk and she has to sit in a wheelchair.

9 The child – Adelheid – is not a suitable .... for Miss Clara.

10 There was a .... on the stairs. It was dressed in white clothes. It looked like a ghost.

11 Heidi wanted to go back to the Alps because she felt
....

12 She had a basket with twelve fresh bread .... for Grannie.

13 One of the wooden .... outside your window is loose.

14 They heard a loud, sharp .... 'Ah! Here comes Peter and the goats!' said Heidi's grandfather.

15 Peter pushed the .... over the ledge and it crashed onto the rocks below.

Writing: rewrite sentences

Example: *Barbie had known Detie for a long time.*
You write: *Barbie and Detie were old friends.*

1 Uncle Alp does not live with anyone.

Uncle Alp

2 You are the only member of Heidi's family.

You are

3 The mountain paths are not safe.

The mountain

4 Grandfather was digging the snow with a shovel.

Grandfather

5 There was snow all over his boots and shoes.

His boots

6 It was so cold the snow began to change until it was as hard as iron.

The snow

7 'Bridget, can you describe the girl to me?' asked Grannie.

'What does

8 Heidi often went to see Grannie that winter.

Heidi often

9 Clara is a very unwell person.

   Clara is

10 Heidi missed her home very much.

   Heidi felt

Grammar: syntax

Put the words into the correct order to make sentences.

> **Example:**   *she could not eat Heidi and became very thin.*
> You write: *Heidi could not eat and she became very thin.*

1 Did the house come into a thief last night?

2 There was a white figure dressed on the stairs which was in clothes.

3 while she opens Every night, she's sleeping, the front door.

4 There was a horse with a man pulled by a small cart.

5 Heidi that had sad Clara returned was to the mountains.

6 They saw a mountain man walking up on his back with the huge a parcel.

7 Her stove had pictures on the room and a warm walls.

8 Heidi spent Clara Peter became jealous when all her time with.

Published by Macmillan Heinemann ELT
Between Towns Road, Oxford OX4 3PP
A division of Macmillan Publishers Limited
Companies and representatives throughout the world
Heinemann is the registered trademark of Harcourt Education, used under licence.

ISBN 978–0–230–03441–9
ISBN 978–0–230–02679–7 (with CD pack)

This version of *Heidi* by Johanna Spyri was retold by Anne Collins for
Macmillan Readers.

First published 2008
Text © Macmillan Publishers Limited 2008
Design and illustration © Macmillan Publishers Limited 2008
This version first published 2008

Illustrated by Martin Sanders and Victor Tavares
Cover image by Corbis/Arno Balzarini/epa

Printed and bound in Thailand

2010 2009 2008
6 5 4 3 2

with CD pack
2010 2009 2008
6 5 4 3 2